Fred & Rose West

Britain's Most Infamous Killer Couples

Ryan Green

Table of Contents

Acknowledgments

I want to say a big thank you to Helen Green, Lacar Musgrove, Prints Magoncia, Jeanine Elizalde, and Valadia Kristoffersen. I couldn't do it without you.
~Ryan

Introduction

On the 24th of February 1994, police knocked on the door of an aging house in the English town of Gloucester. They'd come to serve a search warrant in the case of a missing girl – the daughter of the house's inhabitants. What they uncovered would shock the world: decades of child abuse, an underground torture chamber, and a burial ground containing the bodies of the spent victims of the torture – including that of the missing daughter. The address was 25 Cromwell Street, and these discoveries would earn it the moniker "The House of Horrors".

At the end of the investigation, the number of the murdered was twelve – all young females, including one daughter and one stepdaughter. The couple responsible were Rosemary and Frederick West, and this book will tell you their story. We'll start from the very beginning, with the killers' childhoods and upbringings, exploring in detail the factors that contributed to their later depravities. From there we'll detail the crimes themselves, following the tragic tales of their victims, including the mechanisms that led them to their grim fates. We'll examine how the full extent of their crimes was uncovered in the subsequent investigation. Finally, we'll dig into the malignancies both surrounding the killers and within themselves that drove them to perpetrate their heinous acts.

This book is not one for the faint of heart. It enters into graphic details that may upset those of a delicate constitution. It is a true life report on real events. If you believe as I do that we are better served knowing and understanding the full depths of darkness the human soul is capable of, and if you are able to stomach this knowledge, then read on and discover the story of one of Britain's most infamous killer couples.

Chapter 1 – Beginnings

The story of the couple so horrifically take so many young lives begins in Herefordshire Parish, of Much Marcle, 18 miles northwest of Gloucester, in the very place most of the murders would later take place. On the 29th of September 1941, Frederick Walter Stephen West was born. He was the second child and first son of Walter Stephen and Daisy Hannah West, descendants of several generations of farm labourers. Much ado has been made about Fred West's childhood, and understandably so: one of the most common features of sex criminals and child abusers is having experienced abuse themselves. There is a great deal of confusion around the issue when it comes to Fred West, however. Most of it has been created by Fred West himself through the tangle of misleading and contradictory tales he told to the police upon his capture. Many outlets that reported or commentated on the story chose to take the more sensational allegations that came out of the West investigation at face value, while others acknowledged that little could be confirmed, no matter how compelling the story of West's childhood would be if it had been true to his account.

The entire affair is clouded with a fog of uncertainty, but a probable narrative can be pieced together. Of West's childhood, what can absolutely be ascertained is that he grew up in a large, close-knit family. Despite the austerity of the war and post-war periods, Walter and Daisy West went on to have four more children after Fred. Daisy was particularly close to her eldest son – there was no doubt in anyone's mind that he was her favourite. This manifested in a rigid over-protectiveness, including his being forbidden to date until he was 21. He also had a close relationship with his father, who was far more permissive and provided a strong role model for young Fred. The exact nature and extent of his influence, however, has been up for debate.

In the course of the investigation, Fred West claimed that everything he did was inspired by his childhood. According to him, incest was a common, accepted thing in Walter and Daisy's household, and both parents engaged in intercourse with their children. He would claim that his own first sexual experience was with his mother, at the age of twelve. He also claimed that Walter was fond of bestiality and introduced him to it, and that his father once told him that if he wanted to do anything at all, he could do it as long as he did not get caught. But as we've said, those accusations are not overly credible. We'll examine them in further detail in Chapter 4.

The man who whose vaguely sinister visage came to loom in the minds of the horrified public, started out as a charming blond-haired and blue-eyed infant. He wasn't much gifted academically – he performed dismally in most subjects in school and had difficulty reading and writing throughout his life. This led to a great number reprimands and punishments, which Daisy took personally. She rushed to his defence on multiple occasions, making a row at the school over what she took as personal affronts and as bias against her "golden son." The effect of this on young Fred was likely less than ideal, placing him on the receiving end of a great deal of ridicule for being a "momma's boy" and causing distance from and friction with his classmates.

All the same, he did show some talent with his hands, doing rather well in art and woodworking. This served him well in his adult life, as he became a competent builder. This same skill was also ideal for the hiding of the bodies of his victims.

While he was a rather intransigent and strong-willed young man, it appears that for most of it he wasn't especially violent or immoral. On the 28th of November 1958, when Fred was at the age of seventeen, something changed that: a motorcycle accident. He came away from the mishap with a broken arm and leg and a fractured skull. He wound up with a plate in his skull, the broken leg set shorter than the other, leaving him with a permanent limp. His family also noticed a marked change in his character following the accident –

an increasingly volatile temper, lack of overall emotional control, and a predilection for theft and shoplifting that would continue well into his adulthood.

From these symptoms, it's possible to deduce that Fred suffered brain damage from that accident. One incident in particular, though, stands as compelling evidence of some type of brain trauma affecting his actions. One evening at a local youth centre, Fred was chatting up a young lady out on the fire escape. At some point, he stuck his hand up the girl's skirt, a move which distinctly failed to impress. The altercation that ensued resulted in Fred falling off the fire escape. He was knocked out cold, suffering yet another blow to his head.

His habit of theft reached a small climax in 1961, when he was caught attempting to lift a watchstrap and cigarette case from a jeweller's. He was fined for the crime. The lack of sexual boundaries exemplified in the fire escape incident also culminated in disaster that year when he impregnated a thirteen year-old girl. He managed to get off the statutory rape charge without a sentence due to his suffering from epileptic fits, but it resulted in an extremely strained relationship with his family and his expulsion from their home.

Despite his off-putting appearance and the desperation apparent in both his overzealous advance on the girl on the fire escape and his preying on a minor, Fred actually never had much trouble wooing women. He was, in fact, quite adept at it. His brother Doug later recounted how Fred was the one who always got the prettiest girls. He never left home for a social activity looking anything less than sharp, and he had an easy charm that served him quite well. Despite his trouble with reading and writing, he was an eloquent and poetic speaker.

Following his distancing from his family, Fred West took on several jobs in construction and as a delivery driver. It was while driving that he met the woman who would become his first wife – and later one of his victims. Catherine Bernadette "Rena" Costello, a stripper and prostitute, was waiting at a bus stop when Fred picked her up. He coaxed her story from her: She was pregnant by a Pakistani immigrant bus driver and on the run from her home in Scotland. She, like Fred, had a habit of theft and burglary, and there was an active search by the authorities for her whereabouts. Imagine her consternation, then, when the bus she was riding was flagged down by an officer of the Criminal Investigation Department.

Realizing her need for a cover story, Fred came to the rescue. He offered to claim responsibility for the pregnancy, so that Rena could proffer the excuse that she had come down to look for him, the father of her unborn child, hence distracting from her identity. The ruse worked – the officer let them on their way. With that particular crisis averted, Rena still had a dilemma: she had to flee and remain in hiding. The two of them had struck a chord with each other. There seemed to be only one solution – that she and Fred get married, however temporarily, so that the trouble would blow over. Fred agreed, and on the 28th of November 1958 – within a fortnight of their meeting – Rena Costello became Rena West.

The marriage took place in secret – the West family only knew about it long after it had happened. This deepened the rift between Fred and his family. The caustic character of the bride he brought home did not help. Rena did not fit in with the family at all, and they all saw her as an unlikeable person who was bad news for Fred. Consequently, and once again in secret, Fred and Rena made the decision to leave for Glasgow.

On the 22nd of May 1963, Rena's daughter was born. The child was given the name Charmaine Carol Mary West, since they had decided to keep up the ruse that Fred was the father. Her true father's details were not listed on the birth certificate. Charmaine was clearly biracial, a fact they explained away to Fred's family by saying Rena had miscarried and they had decided to adopt.

Rena's 'bus driver' 'boyfriend' and the biological father to Charmaine turned out to be her pimp. Fred had no problem with this and actually took on a job with him as Rena's chauffeur, driving her between shows and clients. During the day, he drove an ice cream truck, and it was while out on this job that he became entangled with yet another lover and future victim.

While out his rounds one day, Fred came upon a girl crying on the step to a house. She was dishevelled – her clothing in rags and her long hair matted. He rolled down his window and he called her over to offer her a sundae free of charge. They got to chatting, and Fred invited her into the truck to ride along with him for the rest of the day. Grateful, she opened up to him. Her name was Anna McFall, and she was 16 years old. Her mother was an alcoholic and was engaged in prostitution to fund her addiction, which had taken her over so completely that she no longer cared enough to take care of her own daughter.

Fred was moved by her plight and felt compelled to get her out of it. As it turned out, she could help him. By then, Rena had given birth to Fred's first legitimate child, Anne Marie West. With both he and Rena busy and away all the time, the children had no one to look after them. Anne, as he always called Anna McFall, could step in and take on their care. He brought her home and Rena helped her to clean up and wash her hair and gave her a change of clothes.

This state of affairs continued for some time, until tragedy struck on one of Fred's ice cream rounds. On the 4th of November 1965, he ran over and killed a four year old boy with his truck. The death was ruled an accident, and Fred was cleared of any wrongdoing, but his legal exoneration did not dispel the outrage of the community. Fearing reprisals, Fred fled back to Much Marcle, taking the two children with him.

Anna McFall (8 April 1959 – June 1967)

At some point before this, Anne had fallen in love with Fred. Unable to bear being without him, she weaselled his address out of Rena and followed him. This turned out to be a godsend for Fred who, with no one to take care of the children while he was at work, had had to hand the children over to Social Services. Anne resumed her role as caregiver for the children.

During this time, Fred likewise fell in love with Anne. He would later call her his first (and only) true love – he came to regard Rena as neither a good wife nor mother to his children. While they had all been living in Glasgow, Rena had continued heavily in her ways and did not give much in the way of care for Fred or the children. In a journal Fred kept after his arrest, he wrote of how Anne would give him a smile and make him a cup of tea when he got back from work and talk to him about the children. He would also say that while Rena belonged to whomever she happened to be with at any one time, Anne had belonged to him alone.

Their relationship blossomed, and within a couple of years Anne was pregnant with his child. And then, in August 1997, when Anne was six months pregnant, she disappeared.

Anne McFall's death is obscured in a particularly dense pall. It was the very last one to be confirmed as linked to West. While exact circumstances remain unclear, the murder of Anne McFall is the one that is uniformly recognized as the first to be his first. Some of the details can be tentatively guessed at. Rena had visited several times to see the children, once living with them for several months, but may have been unaware of the true nature of Anne and Fred's relationship. With Anne pregnant, hiding the relationship was no longer an option. It could have been that Fred panicked and resorted to extreme measures. Another popular theory is that Anne had begun pestering him to divorce Rena and marry her and, for whatever reason, Fred was unwilling to do so, to the point that he resorted to killing Anne to escape the pressure.

There is another theory, as well. Fred had already exhibited the predilection for extreme sexual acts, which would later become the hallmark of his crimes – something may have gone wrong while he was trying to have some fun, fun that Anne might not have been able to take in her condition. Or, he could simply have killed her in a fit of rage. Without his testimony, what exactly happened may never be known. No seriously difficult questions were asked at the time. When a social worker asked after her, Fred needed to say nothing more to explain Anne's sudden absence than that she had returned to Scotland.

Anne embodied several characteristics that later defined many of his victims: a young, pretty girl living on the shadowy periphery of society, unlikely to be terribly missed. The period between their meeting and Fred murdering her was quite long, but apart from that the pattern would be the same. Fred would pick up his victims at random while driving around on his job.

A chance meeting while on a delivery round was also the way Fred met with his future wife and partner in crime. On the 29th of November 1968, Fred picked up a young girl at a bus stop. Her name was Rose Letts, and that very day was her fifteenth birthday.

Rosemary Letts

Rosemary Pauline Letts was born on the 29th of November 1953, the fifth child of William (Bill) Andrew Letts and Daisy Gwendoline Letts. Both parents suffered from mental afflictions: her father was schizophrenic and her mother clinically depressed. While pregnant with Rose, Daisy received the now discredited and harmful procedure of electroshock therapy.

We can't be absolutely sure that the electroshock therapy had an effect on Rose's tender developing brain, but from her infancy it was obvious that she was not a typical child and may have suffered some damage. She would rock violently back and forth, to the point that if she was put in a pram it would slowly be propelled across the room. This physical tic persisted as she grew older in the form of rhythmically swaying her head, to the point of seeming self-hypnosis, earning her the nickname "dozy Rosie." She was also not terribly bright and did poorly in school.

Unlike Fred, there is almost no doubt that Rose, along with her sisters, was sexually abused by her father. Bill Letts was an absolute tyrant who would deliver cruel beatings to his children that would not stop until his wife interjected – at which point he would divert his violent attentions to her. Harsh physical punishments were also not uncommon. For example, he would compel his children dig up the entire garden for no particular reason, making them do it all over again if it wasn't to his absolute liking.

The one thing Rose would prove to be extremely clever at was manipulating her father. She made sure to stay on his good side and always leapt to do as he said, and as a result would avoid bearing the brunt his worst beatings. She became his favourite – and possibly the prime target of his sexual predations.

Rose turned to a common coping mechanism exhibited by victims of abuse by embracing extreme promiscuity once she reached puberty. By all accounts, it seems that Rose, with time, became an enthusiastic participant in the sexual abuse. She also very early on demonstrated another common affectation of abuse victims: she became an abuser herself, fondling her younger brother in his bed. This was still not enough for her – she wanted more, and with as many other partners as possible. But like other parental abusers, Bill Letts probably saw her as his property and absolutely forbade her to see anyone else. This was no barrier to Rose. She simply made sure he wouldn't find out, going out in secret. This drove her mostly into the arms of older men, who were not always tender. It is known that on one occasion Rose was the victim of rape by an older suitor.

Sick of her husband's constant abuse, Daisy Letts left Bill in early 1968, taking Rose with her to live with one of her older daughters. Yet Rose – probably missing her father's twisted affections – decided she would rather live with Bill and returned to him. It was during this period that she met Fred.

Despite their age difference, or because of it, Rose and Fred hit it off. Fred's sexual appetites were as extreme and voracious as ever, and he was without a doubt thrilled to find someone who could match him in that respect. As soon as he learned of their relationship, Bill vehemently objected, going so far as to visit and make threats against Fred. With a degree of irony that may have been lost on him, he also attempted to have Social Services intervene on his behalf to stop the abuse of his still underage daughter by a man twelve years her senior. Perhaps his concern went beyond his lecherous possessiveness of his daughter and he could sense some dark quality in Fred, the same as that which he had within himself, but magnified to more monstrous proportions.

On Rose's sixteenth birthday, exactly a year after they'd met, she moved in with Fred. She eventually fell pregnant with his child. Together with the children Charmaine and Anna Marie, in the early part of 1970 they moved to a house – number 25 Midland Road, in Gloucester. The Wests' first child together, who they named Heather Ann, was born on the 17th of October 1970.

Charmaine West (22 February 1963 – June 1971)

Through all this time, Fred's shoplifting and theft habit continued unabated. He was booted from job to job after being caught stealing, and around the end of 1970, it would get him into trouble with the law once again. On the 4th of December of that year, he was convicted for failing to pay several fines that had been levied on him for thefts and was sent to prison.

Rose had never particularly enjoyed being saddled with the care of children that were not hers. Her frustration undoubtedly multiplied when Charmaine and Anne's father was put away and she was left with the task of looking after them along with her own new baby. She would take this frustration out on the two stepchildren themselves, very often giving them heavy beatings over the slightest offence. The language of violence was one she had learned from her with a strident, brutal intensity.

Anne Marie would later recount how, no matter how badly she was beaten, Charmaine would resolutely refuse to give Rose the satisfaction of making her cry. This would of course heap further coals on Rose's rage, increasing the fury of the beatings. In June of 1971, shortly before Fred's release from prison, Charmaine disappeared. It's likely that during one of the beatings, Rose was driven into a fury so intense that she killed Charmaine.

Fred came out of prison on the 24th of June 1971. We'll never know his first reaction upon learning of his stepdaughter's death, but what seems likely is that he disposed of her body himself, or at the very least helped Rose do so. Not long after his release, Fred filled in the house's coal cellar and built an extension to the kitchen over it. It was in this buried coal cellar that Charmaine's body was found.

Catherine Bernadette West (14 April 1944 – August 1971)

To explain Charmaine's disappearance, Rose and Fred told family and neighbours that Rena had come and taken her away. But when Rena herself showed up to see her daughter, making that particular fib stick proved difficult, to say the least.

Once again, the circumstances around Rena's death are unclear, but we can guess. Most probably, Fred took it upon himself to do it. The degree to which Rose was involved cannot be ascertained. She may have actively helped Fred plan it. At the very least, she probably knew about it, making her an accessory to the murder.

Like Anne McFall, Rena was a drifter and given to prolonged disappearances. Her absence wasn't difficult to explain. Rose and Fred may never even have had to try, as there was never a missing persons report filed or police inquest undertaken, and her absence was taken for granted by any officials who may have visited the family. And just like Anne, Rena was buried in a nondescript field out in the Gloucestershire countryside, her kneecaps and fingers removed.

The whole affair of Charmaine's death served to bring Rose and Fred closer together. They had a shared, deadly secret now – Rose had killed, and Fred had killed in turn to help cover that up. The cover-up had worked, and the pair was free to continue with their life together.

And what a life it was. They were definitely no ordinary couple, and as time went on they broadened their sexual escapades. Rose began working out of their house as a prostitute, mostly servicing local Gloucester men of West Indian descent. She also placed advertisements in swinger magazines seeking "well-endowed" men to bed her – often for profit, but sometimes just for fun. Fred enthusiastically encouraged this behaviour and may, in fact, have been the first to suggest it to Rose. Fred would often watch her at work through a peephole for his own pleasure.

A neighbour at 25 Midland Road, Elizabeth Agius, sometimes babysat the children for Rose and Fred. She supplied information about the couple's escapades during that period that would prefigure their later crimes. According to her, after they returned late one night, she asked the couple what they had been doing while they were out. They answered frankly: they had been out cruising for young girls – preferably virgins – to have sex with. She took it as a joke at the time. There is a possibility that the pair were perpetrating sex crimes during this period, but if they did, they never confessed.

Elizabeth was herself propositioned by Fred, though she refused, and may have herself been a victim of drugging and rape at the couple's hands.

Rosemary once again became pregnant by Fred near the end of 1971.

Having decided they were a match made in whatever twisted underworld couples like that are made, the couple wed on the 29th of January 1972, and Rosemary Letts became Mrs. West. Since Rena had not been confirmed dead or even declared missing, the marriage was technically bigamy on Fred's part, but there were no repercussions from this.

On the first of June 1972, Rose and Fred's second daughter was born. They named her Mae West. Number 25 Midland Road was becoming too small to accommodate their growing family, so a little later that year, they moved to an address that would go down in infamy and as knowing an amount of human suffering more in keeping with the darkest years of the Middle Ages than the 20th century: number 25 Cromwell Street.

Chapter 2 – The House of Horrors

If the land could talk, if it could tell us of the things experienced by human beings that have passed over it through the ages, there is none that would not have a story of suffering, pain, and bloodshed. Struggle has been the lot of our species, as with all other species – struggle against the elements, against starvation, against exposure and wild animals, and also against each other. There has been no limit to the ingenuity and enthusiasm with which people have inflicted misery upon each other.

The deeper any one place should delve into its memory, the greater the frequency intensity of violence it would recall. The battlefields of the Far East upon which Genghis Khan and his Mongolian horde carried out their campaign of global domination saw so much slaughter they became mired with the grease of decaying bodies. In some cities, rape was so widespread that a tenth of the world's Asiatic population is descended from that one prolific conqueror.

All of Europe is dotted with thousands of dungeons, towers, and castle cellars that would speak of eagerly sadistic applications of torture upon human bodies. Numerous town squares would give testimony of "witches" and "heretics" who were burned or hanged while throngs of spectators, children among them, cheered on – a craze that spread from the Old World to the New. Every place where humans have settled would have a vast library of stories of tribal warfare, interpersonal violence, and wanton cruelty.

Mercifully, the closer to the present we consider, the fewer the places that bear fresh memories of such torment inflicted by thinking creatures upon each other. Violence and cruelty of all types has decreased dramatically with the ages (it is the greater availability of information that makes tales and legends of it far easier to come by in the modern age), and we can be thankful for that. But some places still give setting to such atrocities, which are more the horrifying for their rarity. These places would tell us that while the soul of mankind as a whole has become less savage, there still exists the seed of the blackest brutality in some of us.

Number 25 Cromwell Street is one such place.

The house itself was a drab, brown old three-storey building. It was neighboured on the left by a Seventh-Day Adventist church and on the right by another house of similar construction. The Wests probably had dark things planned for the place from the very beginning: their favourite feature was the cellar, which was perfect for their sexual escapades. Their old neighbour, Elizabeth Agius, recalled Fred telling her that he planned to use it either as a room for Rose to practice her trade, or that he would soundproof it and use it as his torture chamber. Once again, Ms. Agius assumed he was joking, but having had a deeply unpleasant experience with him she could not quite seem to recall, she was no longer sure. All the same, she could not do anything about it and simply allowed the couple to drift out of her life.

It was not long after they moved into the house that it saw its first victim.

Caroline Roberts – The one who got to live

While Fred continued taking jobs as a driver and construction worker, Rose was quite busy herself entertaining clients at their home. She couldn't mind the children effectively. They needed a nanny, and in October of 1972 they found one in Caroline Roberts, a seventeen-year-old girl and former beauty queen. Caroline's family knew of the arrangement and were given the Wests' assurances that they would take good care of her.

If the Wests' idea of care was to incessantly pester the poor girl with propositions and attempted seductions, then care for her they did. It did not take long for Caroline to grow tired of their advances enough to leave, but Rose and Fred were not done with her yet.

On the 6th of December 1972, the couple, by sheer happenstance, found Caroline hitchhiking on the road during one of their prowls for young girls. They seized upon the opportunity to invite her to their home, whereupon they effectively abducted her, bound her up, and took her down to the cellar. Threatening to keep her down there as a sex slave, have Fred's "black friends" come in and have their way with her and then kill her and bury her under the paving stones of Gloucester, they got her to comply with their demands.

What followed was a night of sexual and physical torture. Rose was no bystander, forcing Caroline to perform cunnilingus on her and inflicting her fair share of the torture. Once they were done with her, they let her go, extracting from her the promise that she would tell no one and that she would return the next day to resume her duties as their nanny. This may speak to a certain naiveté on their part this early into their joint career in crime, but who knows: it may have worked for them successfully before. They can't have utterly failed to find partners in all their earlier outings, and at least some of them had to have experienced a stretching or outright breakage of their barriers of comfort and consent. If indeed there had been other girls who suffered at the Wests' hands as Caroline had, then the threats worked, as none of them ever came forward to lay charges.

The Wests' tactic may have worked perfectly on this occasion, too, had it not been for Caroline's mother. She noticed the bruises her daughter had received during their ministrations and patiently coaxed the story out of her. She then immediately called the police to report the Wests.

An investigation was launched and the Wests brought to trial, but when Caroline declined to testify against them, the court's hands were tied. The most they could be pinned for was indecent assault, and all the repercussions they faced were paltry fines of fifty pounds each.

The Wests took the experience with Caroline as a learning experience: from this point on, whenever they picked up a victim they would make sure she could never speak a word of it to anyone – on account of being thoroughly deceased and buried out of sight. And for their "regular" dose of sexual sadism, they would keep it all in the family.

Anna Marie West – Daughter and victim

Fred West's daughter Anna Marie was just eight years old when they turned their attentions on her. The first incident lived on in her memory so vividly that she would recount it in excruciating detail decades later, when her abusive parents were eventually brought to trial. She told of how Rose led her down to the cellar to the waiting Fred and took her clothes off, all the while telling her how lucky she was to have such caring parents who would make sure she would be able to satisfy her husband when she got married. A gag was placed over her mouth to prevent her from screaming, and Rose held her down while Fred undid his trousers and penetrated her.

Anna Marie was so severely traumatised physically and emotionally that she could not go to school for several days afterward. The threat of a severe beating was enough to keep the naive, terrified girl from ever speaking to anyone about what had happened.

Anna Marie would continue to be the prime target of Rose and Fred's abuse until she finally had enough and left years later. Her parents were not the only people who abused her – they allegedly prostituted her out to clients who desired for younger flesh. One of the abusers was Fred's brother John, who allegedly visited on many occasions to have sex with his young niece.

Lynda Gough (1 May 1953 – April 1973)

The Wests needed a nanny to replace Caroline Roberts, and for that purpose they employed another young woman with whom they had developed a relationship. Her name was Lynda Gough. She had dropped out of school to work as a seamstress at a local Gloucester co-op at the age of fifteen. Exactly how she became entangled with the Wests is unclear, but it is suspected that she worked for them as a prostitute out of their residence and was a voluntary sexual partner to them both.

On the 19th of April 1973, Lynda left her family home, leaving behind a note telling them she would be moving to Number 25 Cromwell Street. As an adult, she was free to do as she pleased, but when several days passed without hearing from her, Lynda's mother went to Cromwell Street to investigate. When she got there, it was Rose who answered the door – wearing Lynda's robe and slippers. Rose told her that Lynda had indeed been there a few days but had left to find work outside of Gloucester.

Lynda's mother may have believed the story – that her daughter had moved on. As suspicious as Rose wearing her clothes may have seemed, it was a massive leap to assume that the Wests might be holding her captive, or worse. She was concerned, though, and told a friend who was a police officer about her daughter's disappearance. The police officer later stated during the inquiry into the Wests' crimes that he had made a missing persons report on Lynda but, after an extensive search, no record of any such report was found.

Lynda probably endured a period of torture before being killed and dismembered her fingers, toes and kneecaps removed. She was buried in the ground floor bathroom of the house. Fred, being the builder he was, was always working on some new addition or making some improvement to the house. He would often work long into the night, and must, from the outside, have appeared as just another dedicated do-it-yourself enthusiast. But his constant improvements had another purpose: disposing of the bodies of his and his wife's victims somewhere no one could accidentally stumble upon them. Every single known murder that occurred at 25 Cromwell Street was concealed somewhere under the soil on the premises.

In August of 1973, Rose gave birth to the Wests' first son, whom they named Steven.

Carole Ann Cooper (10 April 1958 – November 1973)

On the 10th of November 1973, a fifteen-year-old girl went out to the cinema with her friends. Her name was Carole Cooper, and she was a resident of The Pine Children's Home in Worcester. She had been given a pass to stay with her grandmother in Warndon for the weekend. The last that was ever seen of her was getting on a bus in Warndon at ten past nine that evening.

She was probably picked up by the Wests during a night time cruise, taken down to the cellar at Number 25, tortured for several days, and then killed. As usual, she was dismembered and had fingers, toes, and kneecaps removed and then was buried in the cellar. That cellar really did prove to be a perfect self-contained ecology for their activities: victims could spend their final agonising days in it then be killed, processed and disposed of without the Wests ever having to lug anything suspicious around in the above-ground levels.

Carole's grandmother reported her missing after she failed to turn up that evening. An extensive police search was undertaken, but it never even touched on the Wests as potential suspects. Picking up young girls at random and under the cover of darkness was certainly serving the Wests well. The reason both of them went out on their late-night trawls together rather than Fred going alone was to have Rose provide an illusion of safety. No young woman with the slightest shred of self-preservation would get into a vehicle occupied by a lone male at night. A couple would probably be, by her calculation, safer. The unfortunate girls who suffered at the Wests' hands probably all entered their car willingly and without any struggle, only to realize far too late the hell they had damned themselves to.

Lucy Katherine Partington (4 March 1952 – December 1973/January 1974)

By and large, the Wests' favourite victims were girls who were drifters, cut off in some way from family and strong-willed, though naive about certain aspects of life. Such girls were likely to disappear to make their own fates at an early age, and so their disappearances would never come as a total shock. Any search or inquest that resulted from their disappearance was likely to be limited and made with an implicit understanding that they were probably be alive and well somewhere. The trawling technique, however, was imprecise, and the next time they used it, in December 1973, their victim would be an exception to the usual way of things.

Lucy Partington was born to a well-off middle class family, a cousin of English novelist Martin Amis. She had completed her secondary education and was a student at Exeter University. Over Christmas, she travelled home to be with her family in Cheltenham. On December the 27th, she went to visit a friend in Pittville, leaving again at ten minutes past ten that evening. She was last seen on Evesham Road waiting to catch a bus home.

Lucy was reported missing the next day, and an investigation was launched. Yet again, as thorough as the investigation was, there were absolutely no clues to connect her with the Wests at all, and the investigation never touched them. While the police and her loved ones were frantically trying to find her, Lucy was in the cellar at Number 25, being tortured for its occupants' sadistic pleasure. This is likely to have gone on for several days, possibly into the New Year, before she was finally put out of her misery.

As usual, her body was dismembered, fingers, toes, and kneecaps removed. It seems that Fred suffered an accident while doing this – on the third of January 1974, he went to a hospital to get treated for a serious cut. A knife matching the cut was found with Lucy's body when it was exhumed from the cellar over two decades later.

Therese Siegenthaler (27 November 1952 – April 1974)

The Wests' next victim was also a high-achieving young woman from a well-off family. She was Therese Siegenthaler, a 21-year-old from Switzerland.

She was a free spirit, eschewing the more formal route of secondary education at the age of sixteen to pursue secretarial studies. In the early part of 1973, she left her home country for England to study sociology at the Woolwich College of Further Education in London.

Therese had an appetite for adventure and travel, and the week before Easter 1974, she left her student accommodations in Lewisham intending to hitchhike to Ireland. She was due back the week after Easter, but when she failed to turn up, people became concerned. She was reported missing on the 26th of April 1974.

Therese had never even reached her destination – she was probably picked up by the Wests in Gloucester or the surrounding area the very evening she left. She may have been offered a night's accommodation by the Wests and accepted, never suspecting the plans they had for her. What happened to her had become routine to the Wests – she went through the same ritual of torture, murder, dismemberment, and mutilation as the others had before her.

Shirley Hubbard (26 June 1959 – November 1974)

The next victim was a little closer to the Wests' preferences in social status, and probably also in age – Shirley Hubbard was a mere fifteen when she was abducted. She was born Shirley Lloyd but changed her last name to Hubbard – though the name change was never officially made. She was attending Droitwich High School and was also going through a work experience placement at a general store in Worcester.

On the fourteenth of November 1974, she left her workplace to head home, and this was the last anyone ever saw or heard from her until her remains were recovered from under the cellar floor at Number 25 two decades later.

Lucy's body showed evidence of what was done to her before she died that most of the others did not – her head was completely covered in tape, with nothing but a pair of plastic tubes inserted into her nostrils for her to breathe through. This was Rose and Fred practicing a type of BDSM known as "close confinement," in which the (optimally, willing) "submissive" has their head or entire body covered up in latex or some other plasticine material so as to deprive them of the majority of sensation and freedom of movement.

BDSM was an integral part of Rose and Fred's regular sex life, and probably formed the basis of most of the tortures they inflicted on their victims. There is, of course, nothing wrong with BDSM, so long as all parties involved are consenting and have set clear guidelines and boundaries for everyone to follow. One such guideline is a "safe word" or "safe gesture," which the submissive partner can say at any time, whenever they feel uncomfortable, their boundaries are pushed a little too far, or they reach their physical limit. The dominant partner must immediately stop whatever they are doing and comply with any of the submissive's directives to release them from bindings as necessary.

Many of the activities involved in BDSM are physically dangerous and can lead to death, especially if they are carried out for a prolonged period – hence part of the necessity for a safe word. Rose and Fred would not have bothered with safe words for their victims – they did not even bother with the cardinal rule of BDSM, which is the consent of all parties involved. It may be that most of the victims were not outright murdered with intent, but that some BDSM activity had gone on for far too long while their bodies slowly gave out. The end result was the same at any rate – several young lives were tragically ended in some of the most excruciating ways imaginable.

Juanita Marion Mott (1 March 1957 – April 1975)

Following the murder of Shirley Hubbard, every one of the Wests' known victims were familiar to them, usually as current (at the time of their deaths) or former lodgers at Number 25. This may seem counterintuitive, as it created an undeniable link between the Wests and the girls, but the type of girl that found her way there typically fit the profile of estrangement from family and a slight likelihood of being missed or vigorously looked for afterwards. This saved them the dice roll of picking up young women from the streets and eliminated the possibility of picking up someone who would be looked for so thoroughly as to be traced back to them.

Their next victim, Juanita Mott, was the daughter of an American service family. She was a troublesome child. At fifteen, she dropped out of school, ran away from home, and took on a series of temporary jobs. She lived briefly at Number 25 but was living with a friend in Newent when she left on the 11th of April 1975, promising to return there the next day. When she failed to return, her family contacted Missing Persons Bureau and the media to make pleas to anyone aware of her whereabouts. Making a report to the police was considered unnecessary – they presumed she had disappeared of her own volition and that law enforcement's resources were better used elsewhere.

The only people who knew her whereabouts were the Wests, and they weren't about to pipe up. Just as they had Shirley Hubbard, they subjected Juanita to extreme BDSM-style torture. With her, they practiced rope bondage, a style sometimes humorously referred to as "two hours of arts and crafts and five minutes of sex." She was gagged with a length of nylon stocking and then trussed up with washing line, forming elaborate loops around her limbs and crisscrossing horizontally and vertically around her torso and head. A length of rope with a noose was then used to suspend her from the ceiling of the cellar. When she expired, she received the same treatment as those who had succumbed to the Wests' lusts before her and buried under the cellar.

The first long interval during which there are no known victims of the Wests was between the years 1976 and 1977. Rose had continued working as a prostitute or entertaining male "friends" the entire time the family lived on Cromwell Street, as well as "managing" girls who worked out of their house. Most of her clientele was still largely from the West Indian community of

Gloucester, but one of her more frequent ones would be her father. Bill Letts indulged in old habits, coming to have sex with his daughter, with Fred's explicit knowledge and approval. Another source of clientele, according to Fred, were Gloucester police, an accusation that was vehemently denied. The accusation, if false, would not have been unthinkable. Rose had a dedicated room – "Rose's Room" – in which she did her work. The room was equipped with several cameras that were used to make recordings of Rose's sessions.

The cameras had all been stolen by Fred, who still indulged his other vice of shoplifting despite the danger of potentially leading law enforcement to his larger crimes. It seems he never did need worry, since that scenario never occurred. Fred enjoyed watching the tapes and also had a peephole into Rose's Room through which he would watch her live at work. Fred's cuckoldry would culminate in Rose giving birth in December 1977 to a child of mixed race, something he was actually enthusiastically happy about. They named the child Tara. Also in 1977, Fred converted the upper floors of the house into bedsits so as to better accommodate lodgers.

Shirley Ann Robinson (8 October 1959 – April 1978)

One of the earliest occupants of the freshly spruced and revamped lodger's accommodations at 25 Cromwell Street was a young Leicestershire-born girl named Shirley Robinson. Shirley fit the profile for the Wests' lodgers perfectly: a troubled teen and drifter, she was also willing to work for her landlords as a prostitute and was eager to participate in sexual activities with them. She was also bisexual, meaning she could play with Rose, who was of the same inclination herself. Shortly before Rose gave birth to Tara, Shirley fell pregnant.

The last that was ever seen of Shirley was in April of 1978. Given that she had managed to stay alive so long, it's unclear just why Shirley was killed. It may simply have been another escalation of the Wests' unsafe BDSM practices. As may have happened with Anne McFall a decade previously, her

29

body might not have been able to cope in its fragile condition. On the other hand, it may have been due to Rose becoming jealous of her. Hypocritical as it may have been given that she had given birth to a child who was not Fred's, Rose may have felt threatened by this younger woman as a potential rival for her husband's love. If this was the case, she may have done the deed herself, or she may have given Fred an ultimatum that either she or Shirley needed to go – "go" being defined in the most terminal sense.

Whichever the case, it was Fred who disposed of the body, going through his usual ritual of dismembering the body and removing the fingers, toes, and kneecaps. The cellar was now full, though – six bodies was all it could take before Fred would have to start burying them on top of each other. Instead, Shirley was buried in the back garden, probably under the cover of night.

Rose gave birth to another daughter – Louise West – in November of 1978. Rose's father, abuser, and sexual partner, Bill Letts, died in May of 1979 of a lung infection.

Alison Jane Chambers (8 September 1962 – August 1979)

The last victim who was unrelated to the Wests was another troubled teen. Alison Chambers was born in West Germany and grew up in Swansea. Early in the year of 1979, at sixteen, she was moved to Jordansbrook House, a care home for troubled girls. She worked under the Youth Training Scheme for a solicitors' office in the city.

The last time she was seen was in August 1979. Her disappearance was reported to the police as an absconder from care. It was simply assumed that she had run away from the care home, and so a thorough search was not undertaken. The assumption was right: Alison had left to stay at 25 Cromwell Street, enticed by the promise of perceived freedom.

The picture of what happened to her was filled in by Sharon Compton, a friend of Alison's who had gone to Cromwell Street with her. Sharon spoke of what drew young girls to Cromwell Street: the atmosphere of family that the Wests projected and the promise of acceptance for once in their lives, rather than constant correction and rejection. But after a couple of weeks, the Wests began to show their true colours, forcing the girls into engaging in sexual activities, including BDSM. Foreseeing the danger she was in from the couple, Sharon left. When Alison realized this, too, it was already too late. She, too, was buried in the back garden.

Following the death of Alison, there is a lapse of eight years until the next murder, at least that we know of. This is not to say that the Wests didn't find other outlets for their sexual gratification. They still had Rose's prostitution business, which continued turning in revenue as ever. Rose gave birth to three more children, only one of whom was Fred's. The other two were of mixed race, sired by Rose's West Indian clients. The Wests also likely engaged in sexual relationships with their lodgers, many of whom worked for Rose in her prostitution business.

The other recipients of Rose and Fred's sexual attentions were their own children. Anna Marie continued as the chief focus of their attention. In 1979, Fred impregnated her, and the pregnancy had to be terminated as it was ectopic, meaning the embryo had implanted in her fallopian tube and wasn't viable. By legal definition, Anna Marie's pregnancy had to have been the result of a rape – she was just fifteen years old – but no further investigation was made into it by the police or social services. The question of the father's identity was never even posed.

The pregnancy proved to be the last straw for Anna Marie. She moved out in December of that year to live with a boyfriend. This was no big loss for her parents – they still had plenty of children onto who to divert their attentions. The two elder daughters, Heather and Mae, received the bulk of the attention early on. The younger ones would receive their initiation in due course. Fred would check on how they were growing and admire and fondle their developing bodies, giving them compliments on how they were "developing." He would also reward them with cream cakes for complying with his sexual advances – as well as shutting up about them.

The eldest son, Steven, would also, around the age of thirteen, be introduced to having sex with his mother, being told it was a normal thing for a boy to do.

The children were also subjected to physical abuse at the hands of Rose. She had not lost a bit of her temper and followed in her father's footsteps in delivering savagely cruel beatings to her children. She often tied the object her rage's hands behind her back with a belt or length of rope and beat her bloody. 31 hospital visits were made by the West children over the years, but no alarm was ever raised. On one occasion, Rose became so angry at one of her sons that she strangled him until he developed bruises around his neck and burst blood vessels in his eyes. He explained these injuries at school as the result of an accident involving a rope around his neck and a fall out of a tree while playing. The beatings were held over the children's heads to make them comply in never telling about the sexual abuse.

Heather Ann West (17 October 1970 – June 1987)

The Wests' first daughter together was less acquiescent and more resistant to the abuse than her older half-sister, Anna Marie, ever had been. Her refusals to have sex with her father earned her the label of lesbian – and she did have a greater attraction towards girls. Nonetheless, the Wests often used expedient of force on her. She was a headstrong and independent-minded child in general, and often provoked the rage of her parents.

It was likely one such moment that got her killed – she drove one of her parents to such anger that they went too far and killed her. Fred admitted to the murder early on after the crimes were discovered, but retracted later on to pin the blame on Rose. Fred pinned nearly everything on Rose near the end, lending some doubt to this, but Rose had already shown that she could be driven to a blind, killing rage with Charmaine. A neighbour of theirs also reported Rose and Heather having a "hell of a row" around the time of her disappearance. Realistically, either of them could have been the one to kill her.

Heather had also told her girlfriend about the abuse the previous year, and the girlfriend had told her parents, who were friends of the Wests. Not believing a word, the parents brought it up with Rose and Fred, who laughed it off. An alternative explanation for her killing was that it was a punishment for this lack of confidentiality, or that they did it to get rid of a "weak link" who could have blown the lid on their disgusting activities.

It once again fell to Fred to dispose of the body, and he performed the usual rituals on her. While he was digging her grave, he got some unexpected help: Steven came out and asked him what he was digging for. Fred told Stephen he was planning on making it into a fishpond, at which point Steven offered to dig it for him. You can imagine his confusion when the planned fish pond was within days filled in again. Fred then proceeded to build a patio over the burial site.

To explain Heather's disappearance, the other children were told that she had left to work in Devon, later changing the story, after a long time had passed with no contact from her, to say she had run off with a lesbian lover. Fred eventually allowed the truth to come out, though, as a "joke" to the children that they would end up "under the patio, like Heather" if they misbehaved.

After Heather, the Wests killed no more, though they still continued with the sexual abuse of their children. In the end, it would be this – along with the (actually truth-based) joke about Heather – that would bring down their facade and reveal them as the monsters that they were.

Chapter 3 – Investigation and Trial

The Wests managed to keep a lid on what was happening in their house for an impressive amount of time. Apart from the couple of girls they picked up who were from a higher social standing, they had managed to keep most of their victims low profile. Even in those two exceptions they escaped detection by virtue of their having no discernible connection to them. They had also, through a combination of intimidation, bribery, and appeal to the common bond of family, effectively silenced their children about the abuse. There had been close calls – making the mistake early on of letting Caroline Roberts live, a mistake they never repeated again, and the breaking of confidentiality by Heather, which she may have paid for with her life.

But what Heather did was bound to happen sometime. Children make friends, and they develop trust and share things with those friends. The only way to completely eliminate this variable would have been to completely isolate their children, perhaps going so far as to imprison them in the cellar as many abusers have done. But the West family projected an outward picture of a normal, healthy family – even if it was one whose house saw visitors at all hours of day and night making patronage of the body of the mother of the house. The children went to school and played as normal, and they made friends there as other children did.

The narrative of normalcy Rose and Fred fed to the children about the abuse may in fact have played a part in their downfall. Telling the children that what was happening was normal and yet instructing them never to discuss it with anyone surely sent mixed signals. They may have begun to view it as one of those "private matters" all families have that should preferably be kept confidential but could be shared with someone they deeply trusted.

In 1992, the Wests' daughter Tara, fourteen at the time, made a friend she

34

trusted, and she told that friend about some of the abuse: the molestation and rape she had suffered at the hands of her father and the mountain of pornographic videotapes of their mother he would sometimes view with the children. The friend did turn out to be trustworthy, but not in the way Tara had naively expected. The friend understood that what Tara had told her was unnatural and wrong and chose to make one of the most difficult decisions a friend ever has to make: whether it was in the interests of her friend to break the implicit bond of confidentiality to get her out of an abusive situation. She made the choice a true friend would make and told her parents about the abuse.

Unlike Heather's girlfriend's parents, those of Tara's friend either did not have a friendship with the Wests to cloud their judgment or if they did they did not allow it to do so. On the fourth of August 1992, the friend's mother went to the police with the allegations, and on the sixth a warrant was served on the Wests' residence to search for evidence of child abuse.

The stacks of pornography were found, along with enough evidence to charge Fred with the rape and sodomy of a minor, and Rose with assisting in the abuse of a minor. The five younger West children were taken into the custody of Social Services and housed temporarily at Cowley Manor in Cheltenham.

The detective assigned to the case was named Hazel Savage. She'd had prior experience with Fred West during his earliest troubles with the law. She had joined the police force back in the sixties when Fred was beginning his habit of shoplifting. She'd also investigated some of his first wife Rena's brushes with crime. Immediately, she began noticing some odd things: first of all was the complete absence of Rena and her daughter Charmaine in Fred's life, and their seeming complete disappearance from the face of the Earth after her previous investigation had concluded. An interview with Anna Marie West, which revealed her tragic story of abuse, also served to deepen her suspicions

35

as she heard of Rose's rages at Charmaine. Second was Heather's absence from family videos after 1987.

The crux of the investigation at that point was the alleged abuse, though, and Detective Savage had to focus her attentions on that. In June 1993, Rose and Fred came to trial for the charges against them, but then the trial hit a snag that was frustratingly familiar: Tara refused to testify against her parents – as, oddly, did her friend. With both key witnesses unwilling to give their testimony, the criminal case completely fell apart. Rose and Fred were free to go.

Fortunately, though, Social Services had enough evidence to keep Tara and her four younger siblings in their custody and out of the Wests' clutches. They would suffer abuse no more. With the trial unsatisfactorily concluded, Detective Savage could pursue her inquiries into Rena, Charmaine, and Heather's whereabouts with her entire attention.

Social workers taking care of the younger West children had heard them refer to the family joke about Heather being under the patio. At first, they assumed that it was a joke and never even informed the police about it. It was only with Savage's continued interest in Heather that one of them thought to mention it. Further questioning of the children left the detective convinced that it was no joke, and that Heather really was buried under the patio. She began to petition for a warrant to excavate the area under the patio to find the remains.

The rest of Gloucester Police had been searching for Heather, but only in relation to the abuse investigation, hoping that she could shed further light that would allow them to press new charges on Rose and Fred and perhaps this time get a conviction. They took the bee in Savage's bonnet over the patio as quixotic, fully buying the Wests' explanation that she was alive and well somewhere out there, and they just needed to find her. The biggest objection to undertaking the excavation was the cost: it would be no cheap and easy thing, and an expenditure of cash and manpower had to be well justified before it was authorised.

As more and more time passed with no trace of Heather, expending that cost began to seem more and more justifiable. The final detail that had to click for them was the fact that Heather's national insurance number had not been used at all ever since her disappearance, meaning that she had never undertaken any employment, claimed any benefits, or visited a doctor anywhere in the UK at all. Either she had left the country by clandestine means as soon as she left home, or she was dead. The only possible lead they had was that little family joke.

The deception comes to an end

On the 24th of February 1994, police knocked on the door to Number 25 Cromwell Street with a warrant to excavate the back garden in search of the remains of Heather Ann West. When Stephen West answered the door, he reacted to the warrant with genuine surprise and amusement – were the police really going to demolish the patio and dig up their garden over a joke? When her son told her about the warrant Rose, immediately telephoned Fred. He replied that he was "on his way."

Fred reportedly left the construction site he was working on as soon as he received the call at 1:40pm, but by the time detectives left the house at half past five that evening, he still had not arrived. He was not seen or heard from until 7:40pm, when he arrived by his own volition at Gloucester police station. What he did during those six hours is a mystery to all, but there has been some plausible speculation. When it was discovered that fingers, toes, and kneecaps of all of the girls and women Fred had buried had been removed, the question arose of just what had happened to them. If Fred had kept them as souvenirs, he may have used that time to get rid of them. Alternatively, he may have visited other burial sites, perhaps that of his first love Anne McFall, or perhaps some other secret site that was never discovered.

The purpose of the visit to the police station was simply to mock the police once again for expending so much time and resources on a joke. His explanation for Heather's disappearance and lack of contact was that "lots of girls disappear, change their names and go into prostitution," reiterating that Heather was a lesbian and had perhaps run away with a partner, and also that she had had drug problems. With the police having no warrant for his arrest, he was free to leave and so returned home. Meanwhile, Rose was also being interviewed at the house, and she would give the police the same account of Heather's absence.

When Fred got home that evening, he took the dogs for a walk in Gloucester Park, together with Rose. Whatever they discussed on their constitutional, it's likely that they both recognised and acknowledged the near certainty that the police would find Heather's remains. Fred also probably offered to completely shield Rose from all suspicion and take all of the blame upon himself.

When Detective Savage and her colleagues came to Number 25 the next morning, Fred had a brief private conference with Rose before instructing the police to take him to the station. When they got him into the police car, he admitted to killing Heather and burying her in the garden, and also told them that they were digging in the wrong place. He was then arrested and taken to Gloucester Police Station.

The Wests' ploy to deflect suspicion from Rose did not work as well as they had hoped, and she too was arrested about an hour after Fred and taken to the police station in neighbouring Cheltenham.

Unearthing the dead

Fred secured the services of a solicitor named Howard Ogden. He was interviewed later on the day of his arrest about the death of Heather. In that interview he gave his first account of what happened: he had been angry at Heather over something, he could not remember what, and rather than quail at his rage or attempt to make peace, Heather had laughed at him. Intending to wipe the smirk of her face, Fred had reached over and throttled Heather. He had not intended to kill her – just to shut her up – but had miscalculated his strength and the amount of time she could endure. He provided a glimpse into his BDSM life when he said that he had endured being choked and deprived of oxygen for much longer amounts of time, and he was shocked when she fell limp as he let go of her.

Nearly all of Fred's interviews with the police and his solicitor were recorded on tape, and they make for a fascinating look into his mind. His recall of every place and setting was vivid – including when the things he said contradicted others he had said earlier. His description of how he disposed of Heather's body was no exception.

He told of how he had taken her into the bathroom and garrotted her with a length of nylon rope to make absolutely sure she was dead and wouldn't wake up when he put the blade through her skin. When asked how he had managed to go through with cutting his daughter up, he stated that he had closed her half-opened eyes. "You wouldn't want someone looking at you while you were cutting into them, would you?" he said by way of further elaborations, seemingly oblivious that normal people don't ever want to cut into other people at all.

He also described in detail the sounds Heather's body made as he cut into it – the worst, he said, was going through her neck, which had made a crunching sound as he sawed through it. Later in the day, the police took him back to Number 25, where he pointed out the exact spot Heather was buried.

Even with Fred's direction, investigators found that digging at the house was far more difficult than expected. It was turning out to be a typically rainy English spring, and the combination of that with the high water table caused the soil in the garden to be absolutely waterlogged. To make matters worse, there was a burst sewer line adding its putrid effluent to the mire and creating unsanitary working conditions. This led to significant delays in finding the body, and when lunchtime on the 26th of February rolled around with still no body, Fred may have begun to believe the investigators would never find the body and give up on the search.

At half past 1 that afternoon, Fred was interviewed again. This time, he recanted his confession of killing Heather. Heather was alive and well, he told them, working for a drug cartel in Bahrain, with a new birth certificate and a personal chauffeur driving her around in a luxury Mercedes. A further interview later on yielded the same answer from him.

At around 4pm, the investigators finally found something – a human bone, in a location different from the one Fred had pointed them to. They may have initially thought that Fred had lied to them and had been trying to misdirect them when he gave them the location. When the police came to him with the find, he dropped the Bahrain story and again admitted to killing Heather. When asked if there were any other bodies out there, he denied that there were.

The bone was taken to the Home Office pathologist, Professor Bernard Knight, who identified it as a human femur – a thigh bone. Professor Knight was then taken to Cromwell Street, where he helped to uncover a more-or-less full set of remains – more, because there were two femurs. Professor Knight, who had a dry sense of humour, quipped, "Either this lady had three legs or we're looking at more than one body."

Fred was interviewed later that evening about the third femur and admitted to killing and burying Shirley Robinson. He described the night he buried her in detail – it was a bright, moonlit night, so he had no need for artificial lighting. He also appeared to express remorse over what had happened, stating that he had a problem and that he had wished he could tell Rose so that she could get someone to help him. He accidentally let slip the number of bodies that were buried in the garden when he said that there had been three victims thus far, before hastily correcting himself, admitting only to the two that were known at that time.

Fred had still not been charged with a crime and so could only be held for a maximum of 24 hours without a further warrant. He was taken before the Gloucester Magistrates' Court, and the police received a warrant to hold him a further 36 hours. Fred was interviewed again after that, and asked a second time if there were more remains to be found in the garden. He finally dropped his insistence that Heather and Shirley were the only ones. He admitted that there was someone else buried there, whom he called "Shirley's mate." This would turn out to be Alison Chambers. Fred's recollection on this detail was incorrect – he had killed Shirley in 1978, while Alison had not moved to Gloucester until early 1979, meaning the two could not have known each other.

On the 27th of February, Fred was charged with the murder of his daughter, Heather West. When Rose was let out on bail that same day, it seemed the ploy to divert attention away from her seemed was working. The next day, Fred had the charge read to him at the Gloucester Magistrate's Court but was not asked to plead. He was then remanded into custody, where he was interviewed about exactly how he had killed Shirley Robinson. He told the police about his affair with her, and that he had decided to end it without Rose's knowledge by throttling Shirley in her sleep. He also described how he had cut Shirley up, stating that he had passed over his axe and gone for his knife to do the deed.

This assertion was not supported by the forensic evidence – Shirley's bones were found to have marks and shatter patterns consistent with having been chopped straight through with an axe. He also claimed to suffer from terrible nightmares over the sound her body made as he cut through it that woke him up screaming. It's likely Fred added these details to give himself a few "humanising" traits. On the second of March, Fred was further charged with the murders of Shirley Robinson and an unknown female – Alison Chambers' identity was still not known at the time.

The Appropriate Adult

Due to Fred's apparent mental deficiencies, as revealed by his near-illiteracy, a social worker name Janet Leach was assigned to him as an "appropriate adult." The duty of an appropriate adult is to assist vulnerable people – adults like Fred, as well minors – through the process of trial, making sure the accused understands everything that is going on and that they are not exploited by the police.

Unlike a solicitor, an appropriate adult is not bound to maintain the client's confidentiality. This meant that anything Fred said in her presence, she could choose to pass on to the police or give as testimony in court. Fred, of course, did not know this, and for some reason he also appeared to have a strong attachment to her, leading to him giving her a great deal of information he would not give the police. Mrs. Leach picked up on this and used it to her advantage, convincing Fred to come out with several truths he would otherwise never have volunteered. She still avoided breaking Fred's trust and never came forward with any information he did not want her to share.

On the day charges for the other two murders were brought against Fred, a member of the public told the police about the former Cromwell Street tenant Lynda Gough and her sudden disappearance. Fred initially denied any knowledge of her, then changed his story to the one he and Rose had told Lynda's mother all those years ago – that she had left to work in Weston-Super-Mare. Unsatisfied with this answer, the detectives told Fred about the ground scanning equipment they had acquired that could sense disturbed earth through solid matter, and that they would use it through the entire house.

Janet Leach was also unsatisfied with his claim that there were no other bodies buried under the house and used the mysterious leverage she had with Fred: she threatened that she would refuse to work with him any longer if he did not confess to everything. This is what seems to have tipped things over for Fred, and on the evening of the fourth of March he handed a note over to the police admitting not just to the bodies buried under Cromwell Street, but to his very first victims from the 1960s – murders they had not yet thought to connect to him.

The note stated, "I, Frederick West, authorise my solicitor, Howard Ogden, to advise Superintendent Bennett that I wish to admit to a further (approx.) nine killings expressly Charmaine, Rena, Lynda Gough and others to be identified." He did not even know the names of all of his victims and referred them by nicknames such as "Scar Hand" for one, on account of the burn scar on her hand, and another as "Tulip" as he believed her to be Dutch (likely the Swiss student Therese Siegenthaler).

The next day, Fred, dressed in an overall similar to those worn by the investigation team, was taken to Cromwell Street to point out the locations of the bodies in the cellar. At this point, Fred's pronouncements began to take a surreal turn. He asserted that he could see the spirits of the women he had killed and that they guided him to the spots under which they were buried, after which they left peacefully. This may have been yet another attempt by Fred to manipulate the investigators, perhaps this time into believing he was insane and unfit for trial.

Investigators undertook the task of excavating the cellar and bathroom, which was by no means an easy one. The cellar had to be dug up by sections, and when one section was completed it had to be filled in with concrete to preserve the structural integrity of the house. In order to get a concrete mixing truck close enough to do the job, the low perimeter wall of the Seventh-Day Adventist church had to be demolished. In return for the courtesy, the search agreed not perform any work on Saturdays, out of respect for that being the church's day of worship. The members of the church also made visits to other residents on the street and held special multi-denominational prayer services to help the community through this troubling time.

While the remains of his victims were turning up over the next few days, Fred was being questioned about the circumstances surrounding their deaths. He still maintained that Rose knew nothing. He admitted to the sexual nature of their demise, stating that he had engaged in adulterous relationships with all of them, but when asked if they had been tortured, he replied with a vehement "NO!" further stating that "nobody went through hell" and that "enjoyment turned to disaster." When it became obvious that all of the skeletons dug up had fingers, toes, and kneecaps missing, Fred was asked about this. He refused to comment on several rewordings of the question as to what had become of the missing bones.

Digging also commenced at 25 Midland Road. The investigators had to break through a cement floor and metal sheeting to get to the coal cellar and then excavate several tons of filled-in rubble. Charmaine's remains were recovered on the 5th of May 1994.

The task of ascertaining the identity of each set of remains had fallen to David Whittaker, a forensic orthodontist. Where dental records were available, he compared them with the teeth of each skeleton, but for several he had nothing to go on except pictures of the missing girls and women. The task of identifying most of these remains proved difficult and painstaking, but that of confirming Charmaine's was one of those cases every profession encounters once in a while, the kind that is both very easy and extremely satisfying, as it clearly demonstrates the inner workings and value of the profession. Dr. Whittaker was provided with a picture of Charmaine and Anna Marie in which Charmaine was sporting a very wide, gap-toothed grin. Dr. Whittaker, accounting for growth, could then extrapolate what the teeth on Charmaine's skeleton would look like and then compare his expectations with reality. It

44

was a perfect match.

As the remains turned up and were identified, further charges of murder were brought against Fred. Although both Rose and Fred maintained Rose's innocence, it seemed highly improbable that all this had been going on without her knowledge, if not her active participation. Rose was also charged with the nine Cromwell Street murders.

The Ghost of Anne

During conversations with Janet Leach, Fred began to talk about someone else who had figured greatly in his life – Anne McFall, whom we described as having been his first true love. When Fred showed Janet a picture of Anne, the probable inspiration for his borderline-obsessive trust and fondness for her was revealed – the resemblance between Anne and Janet was so uncanny that the picture could have been mistaken for one of Janet at a younger age.

Through Janet, Fred revealed that Anne had been murdered – but not by him. Anne and he had been living together, and she was pregnant with his child as well as tasked with minding Charmaine and Anna Marie. He said that he had come home late one night from a delivery run to an abattoir to find his wife Rena and her pimp at the time – a Jamaican man named Rolf – standing over Anne's body in a suitcase. Rena, according to him, had stabbed Anne to death in a drug and alcohol fuelled rage and was still incoherent and uncomprehending of just what she had done when he found them.

With Rena's pimp there, his hands were tied. He could not go to the police. Rolf intended to dispose of Anne's body at the garbage tip, but Fred would have none of that – he said they would bury her at their "special place" in Much Marcle. Two and a half decades later, he followed her "spirit" and lead police to the spot on the edge of Fingerpost Field, where he recalled burying her. He would later admit that he had been lying about the ghost this particular time. When the police expressed doubt over the veracity of this

45

version of events and suggested that it was he who had killed Anne, he reacted badly, stating over and over again that she was not just the first, but also the only woman he had ever truly loved.

In private, he admitted to Howard Ogden that he had, in fact, killed Anne. He also said that he had told his father Walter West about it and even led him to the field where he had buried her. According to Fred, Walter had told him that he would not turn him, and that if Fred could live with what he had done, that would be up to him. He would, however, no longer be welcome in the family home. Fred suspected that Walter had also told his mother Daisy, and the stress of this knowledge had contributed to her succumbing to a gall bladder infection not long after.

When asked about how Rena had died, he said that it had been due to an argument that escalated. The evening on which it happened had begun well enough, with some drinking and a tryst at their favourite field – a different one in Much Marcle from the one he had shared with Anne. During the post-coital talk, she had somehow managed to tick him off. In the course of the argument, he became so incensed as to smash her against the gate, instantly killing her. He buried her in that very field. Again he led the police to the burial site with yet more talk of her spirit guiding him to the spot.

The excavation of the fields took even more time than that of the two houses had. Fred's estimates of where the bodies were buried were slightly off, and investigators had to call in heavy equipment and an inflatable environment tent to protect the dig sites from the elements. The excavations both commenced on the 10th of March 1994, but Rena's remains were not found until the 11th of April, Anne's on the 7th of June.

A shattered bond

The news that Anne's remains had been unearthed brought about a change in Fred. Now that his true love had finally found rest, he was released from his bond with Rose. He did not begin by straight out accusing Rose of anything, but he let slip a few clues: Rose had "always been Anne, in a way" to him, and he had defended her because of that.

Not long after, in another interview with the police, Fred stated, "I have not, and still not told you the whole truth about these matters. From the very first day of this enquiry, my main concern has been to protect other person (sic) or persons, and there is nothing else I wish to say at this time."

Over the next couple of weeks, Fred began to shift more and more of the blame towards Rose. He would begin with an insight into her sexual character: the fact that she had been a willing and enthusiastic sexual partner to her father. He claimed not to have endorsed the relationship, but that he had caught them together at least half a dozen times.

He then went on to allege that the swinging and prostitution had all been Rose's idea, as had the initiation of all their BDSM activities. He said that she had also been a source of shame for him at work – it was difficult to show his face there knowing that all of his workmates had slept with his wife. He also made a further allegation about the incident with Caroline Roberts: he had been a bystander while Rose taped her up and abused her. This was a very different story from the one that Caroline herself would tell. It had been Fred who knocked her out, and both of them had participated in the abuse. He still, however, avoided saying that Rose had been involved in any of the murders.

Once Number 25 had been confirmed as a crime scene, Rose had meanwhile been transferred to alternative accommodations, together with her now adult children, Stephen and Mae. In the hopes that Rose would accidentally let slip that she had been involved in the murders, the house they were transferred to was wired with recording devices. But while Rose and her children did have many conversations, in none of them did she say anything that would incriminate her.

On one particular occasion, not long after the investigation began, Rose had a late-night conversation with Mae in which she gave her version of what happened. It was pretty much the same as the original story that Fred had told – that Fred had performed all of the killings himself and she had absolutely no knowledge of them. When she came to talking about the rest of their sexual activities, Rose said that it was Fred who had driven them both into it all. She pointed out their age difference – Rose had been but a girl when she met Fred, and she accused him of brainwashing her. The prostitution and abuse had all been at Fred's insistence. Rose may very well have meant for Mae to believe all this, and she may have had the benefit of plausible deniability had the children only ever seen Fred initiate the abuse.

It seemed that no further bodies would be forthcoming, and all of those that had been recovered had had their identities confirmed to the best knowledge of the forensic investigation team. There was little else left to do but bring the Wests to trial. On the 22nd of September 1994, Frederick and Rosemary West were brought before the Gloucester Magistrate's Court and had their charges amended to nine joint charges of murder for the ones that occurred at 25 Cromwell Street.

This court appearance was the first time Rose and Fred had been seen each other, let alone been in the same room and close enough for physical contact, since the investigation had begun and Fred turned himself in. Who knows what was going through Fred's mind when he saw Rose. Perhaps he thought she would still recognize their pact and give him some form of affirmation. Perhaps he found himself yearning for old times and wanted to rekindle some of the affection they had shared. Perhaps seeing the woman he had spent so much of his life and shared so many secrets with trumped whatever feelings he had still harboured for a woman nearly three decades dead.

Whatever the reason, when Fred passed by Rose as he entered the courtroom, he leaned over to her and touched her shoulder. She did not turn to acknowledge him or return the gesture in any way. She did not make any moves to communicate with him or even look at him at all throughout the appearance.

If Fred still held onto some measure of compassion for Rose that would give him second thoughts about implicating her, the snubbing he received from her that day wiped them away. He completely turned on her and told his solicitor that everything he had said up to that point had been a lie. The first alleged piece of information he would build this new narrative on would be what had transpired on the night the police issued the warrant on her.

He claimed to have got home and told Rose that there was nothing to worry about and that there was no chance that Heather was buried in the garden, and she had nonchalantly told him that she actually was. After coming to grips with the fact that she had killed Heather, whom he had "thought the world" of, he had resolved that he would have to take the blame for the death. He added further flourishes that painted Rose badly, such as that she had tried to dispose of Heather in the dustbin before realizing she wouldn't fit and cutting her up to bury her.

As he worked to form the story he would tell the police, he claimed, he still believed there was only one body, thinking he could at least explain just one as an accident. But then it occurred to him to ask if there were any more. With the same dismissiveness, she replied that there were "seven, eight, or nine, something like that."

There seems to have been a great deal of turmoil in Fred's mind during this period. Not long after the court appearance, he made the bizarre decision to fire Howard Ogden as his solicitor and took on a partner of the firm Bobbets and Mackan. He may have still been harbouring a dim flicker of hope that Rose would come around. After another court appearance that December, in which she ignored him again, he sent her sent her a letter saying, "We will always be in love... You will always be Mrs. West, all over the world. That is important to me and to you."

49

Noticing his erratic behaviour, prison officers put Fred on suicide watch. The measure did not work: at noon on New Year's Day 1995, Fred was found dead in his cell, having hanged himself using a noose made out of his bedsheet.

The Trial of Rosemary West

Although Fred was gone from this world, his wife still lived, so there was still someone to answer for the decades of sexual abuse and murder. On the 13th of January, after it had been ascertained that Fred had been incarcerated at the time, she had the murder of Charmaine West added to her list of charges. In May of 1995, she officially plead not guilty to all charges, and on the 3rd of October, her trial officially began.

Fred's death actually helped to open up some avenues to the truth that had been closed while he still lived. He had told Janet Leach a version of events that he claimed to be the real truth – and probably was – but had instructed her not to tell it to the authorities. Janet was not bound by law to comply with this request, but she had kept his secret out of a personal sense of ethics. She had come under a great deal of stress from assimilating the horror of his tale, and the added burden of this secret did not help. So great was the strain that she suffered a stroke.

Upon hearing of Fred's death, Janet decided that her promise of confidentiality to him had been lifted and that she could come out with the truth as he had told it to her. The story he told her, given the rest of the evidence and testimony of other witnesses, rings the closest to the probably truth: Fred and Rose had been equal partners. Neither had really pushed the other: when one of them made a suggestion, be it initiating prostitution, picking up young girls, or abusing the children, the other would agree to it readily. Mrs. Leach presented this testimony when she was called forward as a witness. After the testimony, she collapsed and had to be briefly hospitalised.

Another key witness was Anna Marie West, who described in excruciating detail the abuse she had suffered at the hands of her father and step-mother, all the while staring daggers at Rose. She too was overwhelmed by the experience of giving her testimony and took an overdose of pills with the intent of committing suicide. Fortunately, she was discovered in time and her life was saved.

Two other former victims of the Wests also testified: Caroline Roberts, who described her captivity and assault at their hands, confirming it was perpetrated by both of them in equal measure, and another woman only identified as "Miss A.," who described being led down to the cellar by Rose to see two young girls tied up and naked – one of whom may have been Anna Marie.

Rose's defence attempted to convince the jury that sexual assault was not the same as murder, nor did it point to a capacity for it. They pointed to Fred's early confession tapes – the ones in which he admitted to performing all of the killings himself – as evidence of Rose's innocence. When it was revealed that Fred had lied about many key issues, however, the veracity of the rest of the tapes' contents were thrown into doubt.

The prosecution was altogether more successful in building up a case to implicate Rose with circumstantial evidence. They were also able to use Rose's temper against her, quickly learning and putting to use the tactic of making her angry in order to get her to make statements that damaged her own case.

The jury did not take long to reach a verdict: unanimously, they found Rose guilty of all ten murders she had been charged with. The judge presiding over the trial handed her a life sentence for each of them and recommended that she never be released.

There is no punishment imaginable (or rather, perhaps, none permissible by the law) that could possibly repay a debt of ten young lives. Some of the Wests' victims may have been headed for an early grave or an ignominious and miserable life anyway, but every life has the potential for greatness, to make invaluable contributions to society or, at the very least, to be lived in happiness. Because of the depravity of one couple, none of that potential could ever be achieved. At the very least, every single one of the girls the Wests killed had someone, even if it was just one person, who cared for them and was shattered by their disappearance.

Eighteen months after Rose's sentence was read, the Home Secretary would agree with the judge's recommendation and commute her sentence to a "whole life" sentence. The lives she helped take can never be returned, but we can take some measure of ease knowing that Rosemary West will never see another day of freedom in her life.

Chapter 4 – Why?

Take a few moments right now to imagine what it might have been like to be one of the Wests' victims. Picture yourself, for example, in the place of Therese Siegenthaler, looking forward to a couple weeks' exploration of a fascinating new country; or perhaps as Lucy Partington, still warm with the memory of spending time with an old friend you never get to see much anymore since you left to pursue your studies, and looking forward to spending the rest of the festive season with your family; or Carole Cooper, still bubbly from spending a fun night at the cinema with your friends.

Imagine what it must have been like to accept what seemed like a benevolent lift from a man and his jolly, matronly wife, and then to have them turn on you out of nowhere, take you down to a dank, dim cellar and begin to do things to you – things so vile and agonizing you began to wish for the release of death, welcoming its embrace when it finally came.

Imagine you are Shirley Hubbard, Alison Chambers, or Juanita Mott, drawn towards a big, warm family that seems like your first real chance at acceptance for who you are and freedom to determine who you want to be. Imagine your hosts' demeanour towards you begin to change, as they begin to drop more and more hints to you that you would need to do certain...things with them if you desired to stay much longer. Perhaps you acquiesce, and maybe the first few times are even mutually enjoyable. But as time goes on, things become more and more extreme. Maybe you decide you have had enough – but they ignore your pleas to let you go. Or maybe you grit your teeth and bear it, thinking that surely they will let up before they do any lasting damage to your body. As your consciousness begins to fade, you realize – far too late – that they will not.

Imagine yourself as one of their daughters, growing up with the same blind trust and faith in your parents that all children have. Imagine as you grow up receiving weird touches from your father in places that just feel uncomfortable and wrong, accompanied by statements about how you are "developing" that you just don't understand. Imagine being led down to the cellar by your mother and father, being told about how "lucky" you are, before being held down by your mother while your father caused you the worst pain you have ever experienced in your life. Imagine this happening multiple times, to the point where it becomes routine.

Imagine you are Heather, realizing that your parents' version of "care" is not caring at all, becoming disillusioned with them. Imagine venting that disillusionment at your father by manipulating him into greater and more entertaining paroxysms of rage, to the point that he reaches out and grabs you around the throat. Imagine your sense of ultimate betrayal as he does to you the one thing you had always believed to be beyond him, and you slowly faded away...

Anyone with a shred of empathy finds himself aghast to think a fellow human being capable of committing such atrocities against a single person, let alone *twelve*. The question that comes to all of our minds is *why?* Why did Rose and Fred do what they did? What went wrong in their moral development that overrode the most basic, visceral human values we all share?

There is no one simple answer to this question – like everything else that can possibly go wrong with the human mind, it is likely a combination of factors. And because of the uniqueness of every human mind, we will never know beyond conjecture which of those factors was active and to what relative degree each affected the Wests. We can, however, attempt to reconstruct a picture as close to accurate as possible by analysing the circumstances that moulded the Wests, the way in which they conducted themselves and the things that they themselves said.

Could just one of them have been responsible for everything?

In discussions of serial killers, Rose and Fred are nearly always mentioned together, but the only murders that truly count as "serial murders" are the ones that occurred at Cromwell Street. The court of public opinion holds them both as being responsible for those, but given the fact that Rose and Fred both made protestations of their own innocence and fingered the other as being responsible for everything, we should entertain the possibility, at least in small measure, that one of them was telling the truth.

Rose's story, that it was all Fred's doing, is slightly more credible than the other way around. The key factor, and one that Rose herself emphasized, is the difference in age between them. Fred was well into adulthood when he met Rose, whereas she was still a juvenile. He had the advantage of maturity over her and could conceivably have used that to shape her young mind into whatever twisted image he wished.

On the other hand, Rose had a skill that could have empowered her to achieve the same effect on Fred. She had already proven herself adept at manipulating her father and becoming his favourite. Perhaps she realised that she could transfer that skill to another older male. Fred himself stated that he saw Rose as a replacement for his first true love, Anne, and if this is so, it would have made him even more susceptible to Rose's wiles, had she wanted to use him.

Neither reality bears out to the extent of fully exonerating either one of them. It would have been impossible for one of them to carry out nine murders without the other knowing about and abetting them. To begin with, Fred would have to have known if Rose performed the killings, since all of the bodies were buried in his home improvements. It is difficult to imagine the portly Rose shovelling soil about in the cellar and garden without attracting attention.

The testimonies of the children, as well as those of Caroline Roberts and the unnamed witness "Miss A.", all point to Rose and Fred having both been participants in the abuse. As Rose's defence during the trial pointed out, though, a propensity for inflicting abuse does not automatically imply one for murder. But the parallel of their *modus operandi* as sex fiends and abusers with the circumstances surrounding the murders loom too large to ignore. In particular, Rose's presence during the late-night pickup runs had a purpose: to put young girls at ease so that they could take the fateful first step into Fred's vehicle. That purpose would still be expedient in looking for victims to kill.

There is also the fact of the first two murders: that of Anna McFall and Charmaine. One was killed by Fred before he had met Rose, while the other was killed by Rose alone while Fred was in prison. This shows that the capacity to kill resided independently within both of them. The Cromwell Street murders must, therefore, be considered as having been a joint venture between the two of them.

Childhood

The formative experiences a person has when they are growing up invariable bear upon on the type of person they become in adulthood, the course they take, and the things that they do. It's worthwhile therefore to look back into the childhoods of people who commit heinous acts to try to figure out which factors contributed to them, but it is important to remember that nothing is ever clear cut, and that we have to be careful not to draw unsound conclusions or default to the most sensational version of the past.

The most obvious factor to look at would be childhood abuse: the sexual nature of the Wests' crimes points to an unhealthy psychological relationship with sex on both Rose and Fred's part. When it comes to Rose, this factor was almost definitely borne out. Bill Letts' abuse of his daughter certainly had an effect on her, and it is easily seen in the way her behaviour developed as she grew up. The other factor was his temper and violence towards his wife and children, which Rose would also inherit from him. Her children had their own tales of her legendary rages, and it's eminently likely that this was the psychological factor that caused her to take her first victim in her stepdaughter, Charmaine.

Fred claimed also to have been brought up in a sexually abusive environment. All of his siblings absolutely denied this claim, meaning that it was probably a lie on his part. What probably did have some effect on him was the difference in parental approaches taken by his mother and his father. By all accounts, his parents definitely both cared very much for their children, but they showed it in different ways: Daisy West was authoritarian and strict with her children, whereas Walter was much more easy-going. This combination can sometimes have an adverse effect on a child's developing sense of morality: Fred may have received mixed signals from his parents, perhaps for example having a harsh punishment pronounced on him by his mother only to have it lifted by his father. This would have given him the sense that consequences were arbitrary and wrongdoing did not matter as long as he made sure his mother (or any other strict authority figure) never knew.

An important thing to realize when talking about childhoods is that nothing that happens to someone as a child excuses bad behaviour as an adult. Victimhood does not give a person free reign to create other victims in turn. It is always the responsibility of an individual to break themselves out of any negative generational cycles they may have found themselves born into.

Rose and Fred's siblings all grew up in the same environments as they did. Of Rose's siblings, all of them managed to rise out of their abuse and refused to perpetuate it. Rose was the only one who did. Fred's upbringing was not even nearly as extreme, but if there was some negative effect in his and his siblings' childhood, most of them managed to overcome it. He only ever managed to pull his brother John into abusing his own niece.

A short aside – in 1996, John West was tried for the abuse of Anna Marie West as well as another charge for an alleged rape he committed in 1994. On the 24th of November 1996, the day before the verdict on his charges was delivered, he, like his brother, committed suicide by hanging.

In failing to rise above whatever they had experienced in their childhoods, Rose, Fred, and John West (allegedly – it must be acknowledged that he was never found guilty) all deserve the opprobrium that has fallen upon them for the lives they destroyed or ended outright.

Sicknesses of the mind

The next factor to consider in relation to the Wests' murders is whether they were influenced by mental illness. The possibility is one that is borne by a simple consideration of what they did. The callousness of their actions reveals a lack of empathy that is indicative of psychopathy at the very least. Rose's manipulative behaviour, particularly shown by her ability to work her father over into favouring her more than her siblings, is another hallmark of psychopaths: they tend to see other people as tools for getting what they want and learn very early through observation what buttons to push and things to say to do this effectively.

Some form of obsessive disorder, which is especially evident in Fred's behaviour, is also common among serial killers. The most gruesome manifestation of this that we see is the bones missing from all of the corpses. The ability to go through with dismembering human bodies is disturbing enough in itself, but the removal of the victims' fingers, toes, and kneecaps takes it to another level of depravity. This may have been part of a ritual that Fred performed over each body, and it is likely that he collected the bones as souvenirs of each burial.

There is also his obsession with Anna McFall to take into account. In his

58

confessions to his solicitor and Janet Leach, he admitted to killing her, but the reason why he did this was never stated. If it was an accident, the pall of her demise may have remained over him and driven him to seek some way to find a substitute for her. By his own admission, Rose had simply been a replacement for Anne, and she may not have been enough. Killing young women may have been a way to try to fill the void that Anne's absence left behind.

There are also the "visions" that led Fred to the burial sites. It is unlikely that he was telling the truth about them and may have been trying to increase the perception of his eccentricity, but if they were real, then such hallucinations would certainly point to some form of mental affliction.

An interesting thing about the Wests is that for both of them, their mental afflictions had possible physical causes that we can point to. For Rose, it was the electroshock therapy that her mother received while pregnant with her. Electroshock therapy is now recognised as having harmful effects on fully developed adult brains – how much further exacerbated such effects may have been on a developing brain can only be speculated, as no extensive studies exist on this scenario.

With Fred, we have first-hand reports that make the possibility of brain damage a near certainty. Damage to the frontal lobe of the brain – the area right behind the forehead – is well documented as causing the sufferer to lose the capacity for emotional control and the ability to manage their anger. Fred's family all clearly recalled a stark break in his behaviour that was delineated by his motorcycle accident, after which those very typical symptoms of frontal lobe damage showed up in him. Another effect is a reduction or complete elimination of inhibition and sense of right and wrong. The kleptomania that he developed following the accident points to this, as does the belief that his abusing his children was "natural" and a normal thing to do.

The "Family of Love"

That the Wests seemed to truly believe that the things that they did – particularly the abuse of their children – were not only not wrong but also the good and right thing to do deserves examination on its own. This belief was common to Fred and Rosemary both, and probably had its roots in the circumstances already discussed.

During interviews, the West children made mention of a term their parents used for their abuse: they called it their "family of love." Their moral senses were so twisted that they genuinely believed what they were doing to be an expression of their love. They may have explained away the obvious pain and anguish they were causing their children the same way they possibly explained their physical abuse – that it was an expression of their love for the children, and that they really were preparing them for their matrimonial future. This type of thinking is common among parents who beat their children bloody in the name of "discipline," and it seems to have been a small leap for the Wests to transpose this justification onto their sexual abuse.

By all accounts, outside of the abuse, the Wests really did manage to maintain a semblance of a normal family dynamic. They did normal family things, they went on outings together, and they made poorly-shot home videos of themselves, like any other family. In those videos, we see the children interact normally with their parents, laughing and joking with them as children do. They formed a strong bond, to the point that Stephen and Mae chose to live in the family home long after they could have left, and elected to stay with their mother even after the lid was blown on the horrendous crimes that had been committed. Mae, in an interview a month after Rose was convicted, stated, "Family was everything to us, and I could never let them down."

But the instruction to the children that they must avoid mentioning any detail of the abuse to anyone tells us that some part of the Wests' minds recognised that what they were doing was, if not wrong, at the least socially unacceptable.

A deadly confluence

In all probability, none of these single factors alone compelled the Wests' actions, nor did they each work in isolation. They all fed into and reinforced each other to forge forging two wicked and depraved characters capable of inflicting the most heinous of acts.

For these two characters to come together as a couple was a recipe most pernicious. The fact that they both killed independently before embarking on a joint venture of serial murder shows us that each harboured individually the capacity for murder. They each developed their extreme sexual proclivities on their own. But one has to ask: had they not met, would their separate criminal activities have reached the horrifying heights that they did?

Imagine if they had both met partners who did not share their particular mental sicknesses. Perhaps they could have had their appetites reined in and moderated, and they would both be entering a blissful twilight of old age right now, never having known each other and spurred each other on. Maybe if they had still shown a tendency towards violence and abuse, a partner with a better functioning sense of morality would have turned them in and prevented the later anguish of many.

But Rose and Fred found each other, and in each other they each found a dark mirror of their own self that validated rather than tempered their twisted proclivities and created a downward spiral of reinforcement. Rose and Fred truly do deserve to be studied as a single unit, because without their coming together, it is unlikely any of the tragedy they caused would have happened.

How did they go so long without attracting discovery?

The other big question that needs to be asked is how the Wests were able to murder nine people together and twelve in total as well as sexually abuse their own children for a decade and a half without attracting enough attention to blow their entire facade of normalcy. It seems less likely that no one noticed the warning signs and far more likely that those who did failed to act upon them – and analysis of the facts reveals that this is exactly what happened.

Fred West had a history of perpetrating sexual crime long before he met Rose. The fact that this was not taken into account once the allegation of rape was laid upon them by Caroline Roberts is at first perplexing. The inquiry that followed the investigation into the Cromwell Street murders found that without the technology we have today, the ability to search criminal records was severely limited, and even the most thorough search might have failed to reveal anything. What is less forgivable, though, is that a closer eye was not kept on the Wests after that incident. It was a mere five months after receiving the slap on the wrist that was the indecent assault charge that they abducted and killed for the first time – and that first victim had actually been a tenant of theirs who was incontrovertibly linked to them.

The systems that were supposed to ensure the safety and protection of the West children failed them dismally for many years. As big as the family was, some alarm should have been raised over the 31 hospital visits they made. Medical professionals should have been able to tell by examining their bruises that they were being physically abused, at the very least. And yet those professionals did have suspicions, they chose not to raise any alarm. The most heinous case of all in this respect was Heather's ectopic pregnancy. If someone had decided to diligently press her for information about who the baby's father was, she may have broken and spilled the beans. Some kind of investigation should have taken place, regardless, into what was a clear-cut case of statutory rape.

Fred never did get around to soundproofing the cellar to Number 25, which meant that the screams of their victims – including their children's – had to have been audible in the upper floors. The house was never empty of tenants, and if any of them heard screams, then they probably ignored them, deciding they were none of their problem.

The possibility of official – particularly police – complicity in some of the unlawful activities that occurred at Number 25 has to be considered with some seriousness. Multiple witnesses came forward claiming that police officers were among the clients of Rose's prostitution business. Even if they were not, they surely had to have known about it but never moved to investigate or remove the children from the unwholesome environment. An official inquiry into the allegations cleared the Gloucester police department not only of patronising the brothel but of even knowing that there was any prostitution going on. This just seems unbelievably unlikely – a whorehouse next to a congregation of a denomination as highly conservative as the Seventh-Day Adventists has to have attracted some type of complaint.

Another detail that may point to collusion of some kind between the Wests and the police was that for a period, Fred acted as an informant for the Gloucester Police, giving them information upon which they conducted raids on his tenants in search of drugs. Each hand always washes the other in such arrangements, and it may be that the police promised to overlook certain things the Wests were doing – just how much, we will never know.

If the Wests had been stopped after just one murder, it would still have been too many. If they had been able to abuse only Anne Marie among their children just once, it would have been once too many. But they got away with twelve murders combined and perpetrated years of abuse on their children. People like them are still out there today, and it remains up to all of us individually to watch out for them and to raise an immediate alarm the moment we see something suspicious. We could save other human beings a lot of pain, anguish, and loss.

Conclusion

In October 1996, Number 25 Cromwell Street was demolished. Every single brick was crushed to powder and every bit of metal – including the infamous sign – was melted down to discourage collectors with a morbid fascination. Where it used to stand is now a footpath from Cromwell Street to the Gloucester city centre. But try as we might to eradicate the memory of that place, the scars still remain.

Anna Marie West tried valiantly to move on with her life once one of her abusers was dead and the other locked up, but the stain of what happened to her may never leave her. In November of 1999, she would state in an interview, "People say I am lucky to have survived, but I wish I had died. I can still taste the fear. Still feel the pain. It's like going back to being a child again." Less than two weeks later, she would attempt suicide by jumping into the River Severn. She was fortunately rescued from the reeds along the riverbank with a severe case of hypothermia.

Stephen West would joke in an interview about how he was "so much like [his] father", but seriously state that he had decided to break the cycle of abuse. In 2004, he would fail, and would be prosecuted for having sexual relations with an underage girl. He deserves our opprobrium for taking advantage of a vulnerable young person, but it is still sad that the Wests are still capable of creating new victims from behind bars and beyond the grave.

Of the older West children, Mae is the one who seems to have succeeded in moving beyond her past. With the help of a name change and some minor cosmetic surgery, she has managed to create a new life for herself that is not shackled to her childhood trauma. The younger children were moved into adoptive homes and took on new identities.

Two other known victims – Caroline Roberts and Miss A – managed to escape the Wests' clutches with their lives. They, too, live with their own scars and the memories that may never fully fade. But the lives of the deceased can never be returned. The years they could have shared with loved ones will never be lived. The contributions they may have made will never enrich other lives or society as a whole.

But there may have been yet more victims who the Wests never revealed. Fred West's cellmate during his incarceration alleged that he confessed twenty more murders to him that he would release one a year to the police, as well as to a secret abandoned farm where more torture had occurred and more bodies were buried. Being the testimony of a convict, we can only place so much value in it.

But there was a disappearance in Gloucester just after the murder of Anne McFall which seems eerily similar to the methods Fred and Rose would use to harvest young girls for their grisly appetites. In January 1968, a fifteen year old girl named Mary Bastholm left her home to visit her boyfriend, carrying a monopoly set. She was never seen again, and the only traces of her that were found were a few pieces of the monopoly set at a bus stop close to her home.

If Mary Bastholm was taken by Fred and there were others like her over the years, their story may be the most tragic of all: their surviving relatives will never even get the chance to know for sure what happened to them, and except by accidental discovery, nor will their remains be found and properly laid to rest.

About the Author

Ryan Green is an author and freelance writer in his late thirties. He lives in Herefordshire, England with his wife, three children and two dogs. Outside of writing and spending time with his family, Ryan enjoys walking, reading and wind surfing.

Ryan is fascinated with History, Psychology, True Crime, Serial Killers and Organised Crime. In 2015, he finally started researching and writing his own work and at the end of the year he released his first book on Britain's most notorious serial killer - Harold Shipman.

His books are packed with facts, alternative considerations, and open mindedness. Ryan puts the reader in the perspective of those who lived and worked in proximity of his subjects.

Other Titles by Ryan Green

If you enjoyed reading "*Fred & Rose West*", you may like these other titles by Ryan Green:

Harold Shipman: The True Story of Britain's Most Notorious Serial Killer

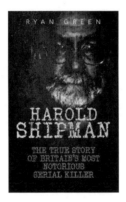

Harold Shipman abused his trust as a doctor and used his position to kill – no less than **218 of his patients** found their end at his hand, making him the United Kingdom's most prolific serial killer by a long shot.

This book tells Shipman's story, from his childhood under a domineering mother to his pathetic death in a prison cell.

We make a study of the man's possible motives and close with a look at the systemic failures that allowed him to kill and steps taken to make sure nothing like his murderous spree ever happens again.

Colombian Killers: The True Stories of the Three Most Prolific Serial Killers on Earth

Luis Alfredo Garavito, Pedro Alonzo Lopez, and **Daniel Camargo Barbosa** are among the most prolific serial killers in the world. Between them, they were convicted of 329 murders, but it's believed that the number they committed is **over 750**.

For these men, rape, and murder were but the beginning of the horrors they inflicted upon the world. The fear their crimes inspire is not about their nature, the methodology, or even the victims. It is about who the killers themselves are.

This book begins with three parts, each dedicated to one of these three monsters of modern-day Colombia. Once you've been edified with the general knowledge of the atrocities, we will delve further into the tiny details, the forgotten horrors, the thousands of ways that we as a society failed these men and, in so doing, shaped them into be the monsters they are known as today.

Made in the USA
Monee, IL
01 March 2023

28947102R00039